Trombone

Intermediate Level

MASTER SOLOS
by Buddy Baker
EDITED by Linda Rutherford

Contents

To access companion recorded performances
and accompaniments online, visit:
www.halleonard.com/mylibrary
Enter Code
3629-2434-4248-1747

ISBN 978-0-7935-9553-2

Hal•Leonard®

Visit Hal Leonard Online at
www.halleonard.com

Contact us:
Hal Leonard
7777 West Bluemound Road
Milwaukee, WI 53213
Email: info@halleonard.com

In Europe, contact:
Hal Leonard Europe Limited
42 Wigmore Street
Marylebone, London, W1U 2RN
Email: info@halleonardeurope.com

In Australia, contact:
Hal Leonard Australia Pty. Ltd.
4 Lentara Court
Cheltenham, Victoria, 3192 Australia
Email: info@halleonard.com.au

Introducing

Mr. Buddy Baker

Nationally known as a brass soloist and educator, Buddy Baker began his studies at the age of 12. On graduating from high school, he went to Indiana University where he earned both his Bachelor and Master of Music degrees as well as a Performer's Certificate on Trombone. Mr. Baker taught at Indiana University as trombone instructor and founded the jazz studies program there in 1959. He also has performed with many well-known groups including Stan Kenton, Woody Herman, Warren Covington, and Henry Mancini. For several years Mr. Baker swerved as a faculty member at the Stan Kenton Clinics and the International Trombone Workshop.

Since 1965 Mr. Baker has served as a faculty member at the University of Northern Colorado where he is the Chairman of the Brass and percussion Department and a member of the Rocky Mountain Brass Quintet. He was recently installed as president of the International Trombone Association and serves as a trombone soloist and clinician for the C.G. Conn Company.

This series of solos was specifically designed to conform with the requirements of the many solo and ensemble contest festivals. They have been chosen so that each piece will present to the adjudicator the elements of performance so necessary to a correct evaluation. The time limitation is also a consideration so the length of each has been structured in the two to four minute length.

More specifically, the material had the following objectives:
1. To present highest quality music from the Baroque, Classical, Romantic, Impressionistic, and Contemporary periods.
2. To keep the difficulty of the solos within the technical limits of this particular level.
3. To select solos which could improve your artistic and technical capabilities.
4. To present in each piece some examples of the principal categories of the grading, such as tone quality, intonation, technique, rhythm, articulation, and interpretation.

Mr. Baker will perform each solo on the recording. He will be accompanied by Ms. Rita Borden.

It is our hope that you will enjoy this innovative approach to music study and development. The care in preparation is of course the prime factor in a successful presentation.

HAL•LEONARD®

7777 W. BLUEMOUND RD. P.O. BOX 13819 MILWAUKEE, WI 53213

Credo

musical terms

legato — connected, sustained style
poco — a little
rit. (ritardando) — slowing down
simile — continue in like style

Jacob Arcadelt was born around 1514 of presumably Flemish ancestry. He spent his professional life working as a singer and a composer, and during 1540-1549 he was one of the papal singers in Rome. After this he served as choir master for Cardinal Charles of Lorraine and from 1555 he served in the courts of Duc de Guise in Paris where he died sometime after 1562. Arcadelt composed many fine Italian madrigals, French chansons, motets, and masses.

"Credo" is based on one of the melodic lines from Arcadelt's mass, Missa Ave Regina Coelorum, a parody work based on a motet by Andreas de Silva. This piece, then, is taken from polyphonic vocal music. The word polyphonic means many sounds or many melodies and indeed most 16th century music was just this: a combination of many melodies. Each melodic line created its own interest and at times was quite independent of other melodic lines. Often in this adaptation the piano part will cover the solo line and at other times the trombone part will seem to go its own way. At all times each part must strive to convey the feeling of direction in every phrase so that the melodies are always interesting.

In each solo of this book you will find, in addition to the musical terms indicating the approximate tempo or style (such as legato), a more specific metronome marking like . . .

M.M. ♩ =72. The M.M stands for Maelzel's Metronome, the inventor of the metronome. This particular marking means that the metronome should be set at 72 and that each click represents the length of one half note. The metronome markings in this collection of pieces were placed there by the editor, not the composer (except for the Kehrberg compositions), and appear on few compositions before the 20th century. The metronome was invented in 1816.

Using a metronome will help you in many ways. The most important benefit will be that you develop a concept of steady time which is important in many pieces. It also will aid you in learning to listen to someone or something else and to play with them. Remember that the metronome marking is only a suggestion. When you are just learning a piece, you may want to practice slowly. Later as it becomes easier, you can pick up the tempo to the indicated speed.

The fact that this first piece is vocal in nature is of prime importance. The basic vocal style is a sustained, flowing, singing approach which is also the most important early approach to learning to play the trombone. From a correct legato style several concepts can develop: control of the air; proper embouchure (mouth) formation; a rich, full sound; endurance; basic slide technique; and the foundation upon which good tonguing is built. Nothing is more important to the young trombonist than a correct legato technique and playing legato literature, vocal in style, is the best way to attain it.

To begin developing the control of the air you should remember the following things:

1. At each breath mark take a full breath (think first of filling the area around your belt; then fill the chest).
2. Keep your shoulders relaxed at all times — don't consciously lift your shoulders — the air may lift them.
3. Strive for a relaxed, naturally free, deep breath. Don't force air in or take so much air that you tighten your throat.
4. When you take your breath, breathe, then at once blow the attack with a relaxed tongue, "TAW". Don't hold your breath before starting the tone.
5. Strive to eliminate the explosive attack caused by a tight tongue and too much force in the air. Starting a tone is like blowing a feather out of the hand — then keeping the air coming! Visualize the water faucet: you turn the water on and the water continues to flow at the same rate — do the same with your air stream.
6. Play a full "mf" sound — not softer!
7. Start each phrase with "TAW", but start the legato notes which follow with "DAW". (Some players prefer to think "THAW" like the "TH" in "THE" for the notes in the staff and lower.)
8. Strive for a quick but smooth slide — don't jerk it!

Now let's practice Preparation 1 and consider these points.

Notice that the metronome marking is M.M. ♩ =96. Set your metronome at 96 and let each click represent the length of a quarter note.

PREPARATION 1

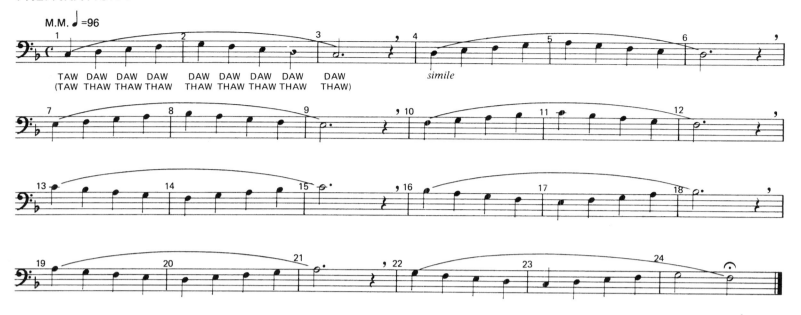

M.M. ♩=96

TAW DAW DAW DAW   DAW DAW DAW DAW   DAW
(TAW THAW THAW THAW   THAW THAW THAW THAW   THAW)

simile

Begin practicing this solo thinking four beats to the measure at about ♩=112. Take a full, deep breath where indicated. You may have to breathe **more** often at this slower tempo. This ( ) means to breathe only if necessary. As you learn this piece, slowly increase the starting tempo up to ♩=144 or ♩=72.

If the air is <u>sustained</u>, the slide is <u>quick</u> and <u>smooth</u>, and the tongue and slide are <u>coordinated</u> (moving together), you will have the sound you **want**. Now slowly increase the speed in Preparation 1 to M.M. ♩=132 — this will take some practice.

Measures 1-12 Start the piece with an easy "mp" sound and <u>sustain</u> that first long phrase with plenty of air. The second phrase becomes more intense in measures 10 and 11 so convey the idea that the phrase is beginning to move forward.

The slight crescendo beginning in measure 9 will help this motion.

Measures 13-20 The sound continues to build in intensity. Don't let the volume drop below "mf" until measure 20.

Measures 21-34 Again keep the volume up to "mf".

Measures 35-46 You will notice that the "F" in measure 39 is to be played in 6th position. In many other pieces you will find this <u>alternate position</u> to be most useful. It will help you play with better connection and speed at times. Practice Preparation 2 to learn the sound and feel of this "F" in 6th position. The "F" in 6th position will be very close to the "C" below (perhaps the "F" will be a bit shorter). Let your ear "tell" your arm what to do.

PREPARATION 2

M.M. ♩=80

Measures 47-53 Keep the air moving throughout the phrases. Relax only at the end of the phrase (in this case measures 52 and 53).

Measures 54-63 Make the contrast between the "mf" in measures 54-60 and the "p" at the end of measure 60 noticeable so it will be a surprise to the listener.

Measures 64-72 The intensity of this phrase reaches a peak in measure 67. Keep the sound full and intense through measure 69. After this point the sound can begin to relax and die away.

Strive for long, floating phrases in this piece. It should <u>not</u> sound like a march! There should be no stressed notes, rather, each phrase should be carefully shaped with all the smoothness and connection you can attain — "sing" it. Observe your dynamics carefully, they are different than the piano dynamics at times.

Credo

Jacob Arcadelt
(1514-1562)

I Said, "I Will Forget Thee"

musical terms

sostenuto — sustained and connected
expressive (often written expressivo) — with feeling and emotion
animato — animated, with life, usually slightly faster, moving
tempo I — return to original tempo

Johannes Brahms was born in Hamburg, Germany, in 1833. He spent most of his life in Vienna, an accomplished pianist, conductor, and composer. His compositions include several large orchestral and choral works plus many chamber, piano, and organ works and nearly 200 solo songs (from which this song was taken). Brahms died in Vienna in 1897, one of the most important composers of all times and perhaps the most important composer of the 19th century.

This song, taken from a solo song for bass voice and piano, shows some of the lyric, expressive qualities present in most of the music Brahms wrote. This particular song was first published in 1864, a musical setting of a poem "Nicht mehr zu dir zu gehen" by the poet Daumer.

This melody must convey warmth and a lyric, expressive style. Vibrato can add a great deal to this solo if it is done properly. Vibrato is the fluctuating or pulsating effect you hear, especially on the longer tones. It is an essential technique for a good trombonist, but should be used only after a full, rich tone quality has already been established.

Two methods of producing vibrato are recommended for the trombonist: the movement of the slide or the movement of the jaw. It is suggested that you start with jaw vibrato because it tends to keep the lower jaw, tongue, embouchure, and throat relaxed. Jaw vibrato is produced by moving the jaw in a "chewing motion". As you begin to develop your vibrato, remember the following things:

1. It is important that you not use vibrato except where needed — many teachers feel it is best to warm up and do your daily basic exercises with a pure, straight sound with no vibrato.
2. Keep the air moving through the horn when you begin moving the lower jaw. Resist the temptation to stop blowing when the lower jaw begins to move!
3. At first overdo the jaw movement. It will sound strange to you, but this is necessary to get the feeling of using the proper jaw muscles. Try to copy the vibrato demonstrated on the tape. The vibrato should not be too wide (width of variation above and below pitch), but it must be wide enough to be heard. Also, the vibrato should not be too fast (sounds nervous) or too slow (sounds unrefined and can cause intonation problems). Listen to fine soloists (instrumental and vocal) and try to copy their vibrato. It will take time to produce a consistent, beautiful vibrato.

PREPARATION 3

The metronome marking at the beginning of this solo is designed to give you only a general idea of the speed of the solo. It should not be practiced with metronome since it is music that should not have a steady beat throughout (characteristic of most 19th century, Romantic, music). Notice several ritardando (rit.) indications and the animato and Tempo I markings. This indicates that the music must be free and lyric as you will hear on the tape. Also, you will notice that the piece is very slow — so slow that it is suggested that you count it in eighth notes (1 and 2 and 3 and).

Unlike the "Credo", this 19th century selection has notes of stress indicated by a dash over the note ( ). Give these notes full value and a bit more weight with your breath — they are important notes in the phrase and should be stressed to create a more expressive, personal style.

Measures 1-12 Each of the short phrases must be shaped properly. One way this shape is indicated is by the dynamic markings ( ). Build each of these phrases to the peak in measure 6 and then relax each phrase through measure 12.

Measures 13-24 This section has a little more movement than the first section. In measure 13 play the "C" to "Bb" movement without tonguing — a natural slur. The "Bb" to "A" and the "A" to "G" must be played with a legato tongue to prevent a "smear". In the same measure play the "G" to "F" with a natural slur (no tongue). Remember that you should use a natural slur wherever you can and try to duplicate this sound with legato tonguing.

In measure 17 you have a new rhythm, a dotted eighth and sixteenth. Divide the beat into four parts and think of the dotted eighth as three tied sixteenth notes. Practice Preparation 4 to help you set this in your mind.

PREPARATION 4

Also, notice that some of the "D's" above the staff are indicated to be played in the 4th position which is slightly long (+4). Your ear must guide you in finding exactly where this particular 4th position is. Preparation 5 will help you locate this alternate position for "D". Using a few alternate positions will help you, especially in solo work, with connection and speed but when you're playing loudly ("f" or more) it is suggested you always use the "home" or regular positions for a fuller, more secure sound.

PREPARATION 5

Measures 25-28 With the return of the original tempo, the melodic material is similar to that at the beginning of the solo. Think of the form of the piece as being A (measures 1-12), B (measures 13-24) during which time the peak of the piece is reached in measure 17, and A (measures 25-38).

This is music from the 19th century (the Romantic era). It must be expressive and lyric and it must reflect a great deal of your particular personality. Strive to communicate something of yourself in the song.

I Said, "I Will Forget Thee"

Vittoria! Vittoria!

musical terms

allegro con brio — lively with vigor
piu lento — a little slower
tempo primo — return to the first tempo
c. or ca. (circa) approximately
marcato — marked, emphatic — usually indicated by

Although Giacomo Carissimi (c. 1604-1674) spent the greater portion of his professional life composing church music in Rome, he played an important part in the cultivation of the solo cantata. He is also noted for his developments in recitative writing especially in his **oratorios**, often rather dramatic in treatment.

This vocal piece originally for bass voice and piano, is a good example of the straightforwardness of Carissimi's melodic style and is arranged here with contrasting sections of marcato and legato style.

You will find that this selection is easy to memorize and it will make a good early contest piece as it displays a full sound and contrasting styles.

Measures 1-23 The piece begins with the marcato section. Play this slightly accented and with a full sound and a relaxed "TAW" for the notes in the staff, changing to a "TUH" for the notes above the staff. Begin learning the piece at a metronome marking of about ♩=96 then move on to ♩=132 as the piece becomes easier. There should be a slight rit. in measures 35 and 36.

Be sure to observe the dynamics carefully because the solo and accompaniment parts quite often have different marks at the same place. Use these dynamics to create a lot of interest in the music.

Measures 24-36 In measure 25 and in several other places there are alternate positions indicated. Use them even if you are having difficulty getting them in tune. With practice your ear will eventually "tell" your arm what to do.

The groupings of notes in measures 25 and 26 can be accomplished in the following manner. Preparation 6 shows how the tongue should work. The main thing to strive for is evenness. If necessary, practice them slower at first to get them under control.

PREPARATION 6

M.M. ♩=96-132

mf TUH TUH TUH DUH TUH DUH TUH DUH TUH DUH TUH DUH TUH DUH TUH TUH

Measures 36-55 At the piu lento (last beat of measure 36) the style of the piece changes somewhat. Rather than the marcato style, each note here is tongued with a "TAW" ("TUH" above the staff) but with a more relaxed tongue and <u>not so much</u> weight with your air on each note. Tongue each note but play them in a more connected fashion and KEEP THE AIR FLOWING through the **phrase**. This section should also slow down a little.

Measures 56-69 At measure 56 return to the original tempo — faster and with a more marcato style (a change of tempo and style). Remember to play the marcato style with a full sound and much energy.

Measures 70-81 This piece ends with great energy so hold your last note in measure 77 full value at a "f" level with no diminuendo. Likewise the pianist should play "f"

to the end of the piece. Again work out the eighth note passages — slowly if necessary.

The last section may be repeated if desired. It is recommended that you take the repeat if you are playing this selection as a competition piece.

There are many things concerning performance of the piece which should be communicated, but all things about music certainly cannot be explained or described verbally. Music indeed is a very special kind of expression and communication. You will learn a great deal from listening to the tape and you, no doubt, will get ideas which you may wish to try, giving the piece a more "personal" touch. This piece should <u>sound</u> like it's fun to play — convey a happy, energetic spirit when you perform it!

Vittoria! Vittoria!

Giacomo Carissimi
(c. 1604-1674)

Modal Moods

musical terms

st. mute (straight mute) — use mute to play this section
open — take mute out of horn
dolce — sweetly
molto accel. (molto accelerando) — very much faster and faster in tempo
declamando — in a loud, heavy, impressive style
grad. (gradual) — little by little
dim. (diminuendo) — get softer
sub. (subito) — suddenly
a tempo — in tempo, in time, return to the tempo predeeding a rit.
mfsp — attack the note with weight at "mf" and become suddenly soft ("p")

new note

F#

Very short
3rd Position

Robert Kehrberg began doctoral work in trombone pedagogy and composition at the University of Northern Colorado during the fall of 1975. He has taught in the public schools in Nebraska and has played and taught trombone for many years. Bob understands the challenges confronting the young trombonist and is qualified to compose music which is at once musically interesting yet provides many learning opportunities of appropriate difficulty for this level.

This is a <u>contemporary</u> piece of music — music from the <u>present</u> period of time, written in 1976. Contemporary music, in general, has several characteristics not found in most music written earlier than the 20th century. Specifically, <u>expect</u> to confront some of the following:

1. Many times no key signature is indicated and all accidentals are written in. This piece has a key signature, but you'll notice it also has many accidentals.

2. Use of extreme dynamic levels. You will find "p" to "ff" in this selection.
3. Unusual or wide intervals. Intervals as large as major sevenths are used in "Modal Moods".
4. Extreme registers. This work includes "F" below the staff to "F#" above the staff.
5. Unusual rhythm patterns and unusual combinations of rhythms. In measure 32 you'll see ♪♩ ♫ ♫ (the beat is divided into 2, 3, and 4 parts).
6. Use of different tone colors. Here the straight mute is required. This mute tends to cause your pitch to go high (sharp). Expect to have to <u>lengthen</u> your slide positions slightly when you use the straight mute. Tune your instrument to the piano <u>without</u> the mute.
7. Use of more unusual scales or modes. "Modal Moods" is based on two modes, the B phrygian mode and the C mixolydian mode. Study and play these as shown in Illustration 1 to get the sound in your ear.

ILLUSTRATION 1

B PHRYGIAN MODE   C MIXOLYDIAN MODE

All of the notes in Preparation 7 are in this piece. Find where they are — let your ear guide you. Also, get all the way out to 7th position. Many young students never get there. Move your shoulder forward as you reach for 7th position and let your thumb come off of the slide bar — REACH! Also, don't puff your cheeks for the low notes. Keep the corners of your mouth gently firm and DROP your lower jaw to produce the low register. Low notes require more air than higher notes, but move the air evenly and don't force it. Think a big, slow, even stream of air for the low register and take plenty of air when you inhale.

PREPARATION 7

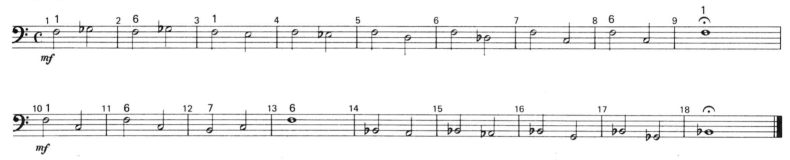

Measures 1-30 There are two elements which may seem slightly confusing — the "melodies" and the rhythm. In this solo as in much of contemporary music, the "melodies" are not especially "tuneful". Get used to the intervals and the sounds in this piece by practicing slowly and listening carefully.

Count throughout the piece so the rhythms will not be so confusing. When you are putting both the solo and accompaniment together, it is even more important that you count. The illustration shows some of the note values and rhythms to which you should pay particular attention. The piano rhythm cues will also help guide you.

ILLUSTRATION 2

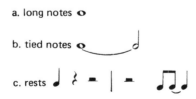

Measures 31-39 In measure 32 you have two new rhythms. The first is a sixteenth note followed by a dotted eighth. Divide the note into four parts and think of the dotted eighth as the last three sixteenths tied. The second rhythm is a triplet which divides a quarter note beat into three equal parts.

♩ = ♪♪♪ Practice the following exercise using these two rhythms.

PREPARATION 8

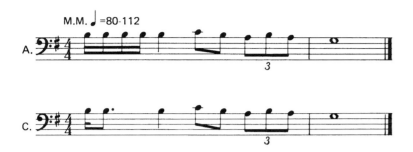

In measure 37, "C" is indicated to be played in 6th position even if you have an F attachment or trigger. If you have no trigger, of course, you have no choice. The reason for this is that it is easier to execute large ascending (going up) intervals by coming in with the slide. The extra pressure created in the horn will help you to securely produce the top note. Also, there is not the danger of sounding unwanted notes between the two written notes of the interval.

In measure 41 there are four sixteenth notes that should be played with detached tonguing. Preparation 9 will help you get the feel of this faster staccato tongue. The main thing to remember when practicing this exercise is to keep the air moving faster through the horn as the tongue moves faster. The tongue should "say" TAW-TAW-TAW-TAW on the sixteenth notes, NOT TAWT -TAWT-TAWT-TAWT. In the last case, the tongue is returning to cut off the sound too soon. This produces a dry, brittle sound which is not pleasing to the ear..On the following exercise, play a nice full half note then keep the air moving as you add the tongue for the sixteenth notes. Start this exercise at ♩=80 and slowly increase the tempo to ♩=120 (slightly faster than the tempo of the first section in this piece).

PREPARATION 9

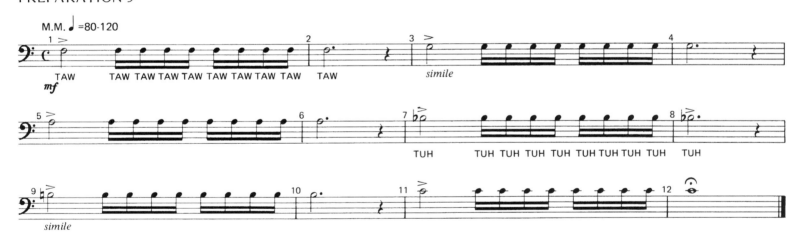

Measures 51-89 In measures 57 and 58 pay attention to the positions and listen carefully.

Measures 90-104 The melodic ideas of the beginning of the solo return in this section. Keep in mind the ideas discussed earlier. Gradually diminuendo to make the song sound finished.

The high "F#" in measure 72 is always played in a very short 3rd position (--3). Keep the air moving a bit faster through the fast notes ( ). Observe the dynamics carefully in this section to bring out the intensity and interest. Be sure to play the "ff" with a big, full sound but not so loud that it becomes ugly and distorted.

Listen to the performance of this selection several times to get the sound of the piece in mind. You'll need to know the piano part pretty well before you will be successful playing with the tape. The composition is not really a solo with an accompaniment, it is more like a duet (both parts are equally important most of the time and at times the piano part is more important than the trombone part). The pianist must be proficient.

Modal Moods

Sarabande and Menuett

musical terms

sarabande — an early dance in slow 3/2 or 3/4 time
menuett (minuet) — an early French dance in a moderate 3/4 time
cantabile — in a singing style
Baroque — a term used to describe the lavish architectural (and musical) style of the
17th century and early 18th century

new note

G

Very short
2nd Position

George Frederic Handel was born in Halle, Saxony in 1685 and spent the greater portion of his professional life composing music. Among his compositions are operas, oratorios, passions, and many other secular choral works and church music. Handel also wrote considerable orchestral and chamber music as well as suites for harpsichord and numerous songs. He died in 1759 in London, well accepted and one of the most important composers of the late Baroque period.

These two dance movements were taken from a collection of pieces (isolated dance movements) for alto recorder and were usually accompanied by harpsichord and cello or bassoon. The Baroque instrumental music, then, has a distinct sound: a higher solo voice, a lower "melodic line" (called the basso continuo part), and a light harmonic filler between these two melodic lines (originally played on harpsichord but now usually played on piano). This solo was recorded with trombone, piano, and a cello playing the basso continuo part so that you could hear this Baroque sound. Although much of the Baroque quality will be lost if the cello (or bassoon) is not used, the piano can play this part as well. The pianist should strive to bring out this continuo melody. In any case the pianist should play the middle voices very lightly. A separate cello or bassoon part has been included if you want to have a friend play with you.

This music must be performed with a certain beauty and grace characteristic of most late Baroque music. Work for long phrases and don't break them if possible. If you can leave out some of the optional breaths indicated in the middle of phrases with parentheses, do so. The dynamics will help add direction and interest to the phrase which should be played as connected (legato) and song-like as possible. The piano interludes will give you a chance to rest.

Measures 1-16 You will find several "D's" above the staff to be played in a sightly long 4th position (+4) and a new alternate position in measure 11: "F" above the staff in a slightly shorter 4th position (-4). Preparation 10 will help you "find" the correct slide position for those notes. Play this exercise before you play this piece to develop security with these alternate positions. The three alternate positions you have learned so far are the three most important to the intermediate student — learn where they are and use them. Don't be afraid of them!

PREPARATION 10

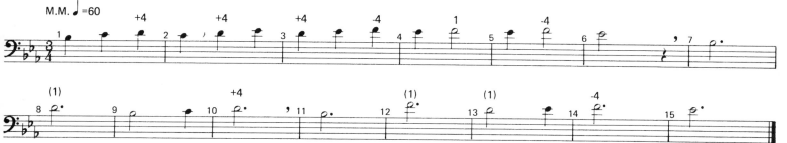

In measure 13 you have a new note, high "G". This pitch seems to be a problem for many young trombonists as far as intonation is concerned (your tuning or exact pitch on this note). Most young trombonists tend to play it flat (low). Preparation 11 will help you to "find" this "G" — it's a very short 2nd position (--2). Follow this procedure: (1) sit at the piano and first tune your middle "Bb" to the piano. (2) play on the piano the chord at the beginning of Preparation 11 with the sustaining pedal down. (3) play Preparation 11 on the trombone letting the piano chord continue to sound. Are you in tune with the piano "G"?

PREPARATION 11

Measures 17-28   In this section the accompaniment picks up the same melody that the soloist played in measure 5. It should be performed in the same style — very connected and lyrical. Remember: the bottom piano part is also an important melody that should be brought out. The soloist must be sure to keep counting during these measures so the entrance will be accurate.

Measures 29-40   With the change in the melodic line in this measure the dynamic level should be slightly louder. Take in plenty of air (not so much that you tighten your throat) before each phrase. As you become more familiar and improve your breath control, strive to play the phrases leaving out the optional breath marks.

Measures 1-8   There should be a slight break between the two dances as they are separate pieces. Most performers would pause for a brief moment of silence, breathe, and proceed with the "Menuett". The "Menuett" should show a different style than the "Sarabande". It is faster and each note is pronounced with a "T" in the tongue — connected, but tongued lightly.

Measures 9-16 Here again the accompaniment has the melody. Be sure to bring out the top and bottom lines and play in the same style as the trombone did earlier.

Measures 17-24   Notice the shape of this section. It builds to a "f" in measure 21 and stays at this dynamic level through measures 21, 22, and 23. Beginning in measure 24 let the dynamic level decrease slightly to complete the phrase.

Measures 25-33   As a contrast to the light, tongued style, this section should be much more legato. The sudden soft beginning of this section provides some interest to the solo. Gradually let the volume build to a full, solid "f". The poco rit. the last time should not be overdone. If the piece were to slow down too much, it would lose its effectiveness.

Sarabande and Menuett

George Frederic Handel
(1685-1759)

Gloria

musical term

segue — proceed without a break

"Gloria" is one of the four vocal parts from the mass, Missa Noe Noe, written by Jacob Arcadelt (from whose work the "Credo" was also taken). Missa Noe Noe is a parody mass based on a motet by Jean Mouton.

This piece may be an endurance problem for a young player. Meet this challenge by breathing deeply and supporting your air stream from below your rib cage (at your beltline). If you use your upper chest muscles to blow the air, you'll experience tightness in your throat, tongue, and embouchure. Go after the higher notes with gently firm corners and AIR. Don't depend on tongue and mouthpiece pressure to get higher notes! Rest when your embouchure (mouth) is tired. If you can play this selection (up to tempo) and play all of the "G's" with relative ease, then you can be sure that you are beginning to use your embouchure and your AIR correctly.

Measures 1-19 When played up to tempo, this piece has several tricky rhythms (see measures 7, 8, and 11 — the ties and dotted quarter note in the middle of the measure can catch you if you're not counting in your mind). Begin learning the piece at about ♩ =112. At this tempo you will have to take a few extra breaths and you should rest before you start on measure 61. Gradually, after you have learned to play

the rhythms correctly, increase the speed to ♩ =152, then begin to feel it in two beats per measure ♩ =76 which is the same speed as ♩ =152.

Again you have several "G's" in this selection. Listen carefully to get these notes in tune. (remember: a very short 2nd position). Practice Preparation 11 again to check this out. As you approach the "G's" above the staff your legato tongue may feel more like "Di" with the "i" sounding like the "i" in "it". Don't allow your tongue to get up into a "Dee" feel. This may cause tightness in your tongue and throat — "Dǐ" not "Dee" for the high legato ("Tǐ" not "Tee" for high staccato tonguing).

Use the compression in the slide (come in with the slide) for large ascending (up) intervals. In measure 13, even though it is possible to play the high "G" in 4th position, play it in -- 2nd. This movement of the slide in will help you produce the high "G" with less embouchure energy and in addition you have a better chance of not getting extra unwanted pitches between the two "G's". Preparation 12 will help you feel how this slide compression works.

PREPARATION 12

Measures 20-31   Dynamics are often <u>different</u> in the trombone and piano parts. Carefully play what is indicated — work for the independence of line characteristic of this 16th century music. Notice that this section reaches a peak in measure 28. Keep your air moving as you approach the "G". Blow through the "G" and the measure and then begin to relax your support slightly.

Measures 32-60   This section has several "G's" which are the high points of the phrases. Play them with air blown from the beltline. You should also experience a slight lift in the chest when you play high notes.

Measures 61-79   Again, use the compression of the slide on the movement in measure 67, (play the top "G" in a very short 2nd position).

Measures 80-97   Keep up the breath support in this section. You are playing in the higher register for quite a while. If you experience fatigue in your embouchure, take that deep breath and depend upon your blowing muscles (below your rib cage) to do the work of sustaining the sound.

Measures 98-109   Notice that this piece does not close with a full, strong sound. The last moderately loud phrase occurs in measures 100 and 101. From then on the sound and energy die away to the end of the piece. Again, don't ritard. too much at the end.

In its final form, this piece must flow along in two beats per measure. The phrases are long and must be well shaped — no stress on individual **notes**. Vibrato will add beauty but don't use too much. At the **segue**, only a slight ritard. and a good breath are needed — don't make much of a break. This is really <u>one</u> piece with two sections.

Use this piece not only as a solo piece, but also as a piece to help you develop your counting, intonation, alternate positions, breathing, and embouchure. If you can execute this piece with ease, your basics are coming along well.

Gloria

Jacob Arcadelt
(1514-1562)

Largo and Allegro

musical terms

largo — slow and broadly
allegro — lively
+ — signifies that some sort of appropriate ornament is to be added to this note

new note

Ab   3rd Position

These two movements, "Largo and Allegro", were taken from one of Handel's early flute sonatas. They were originally composed so that the "Largo" section actually served as a slow introductory section to the "Allegro" and this relationship is retained in this transcription.

Typical of most Baroque instrumental music is the ornamentation found in these two movements. This ornamentation or decorating of the melodic line seemingly came into existence for several reasons: (1) to create intensity in the melodic line by using pitches not common to the accompanying harmony (non-chord tones), (2) to "fill in" larger intervals in the slower movements, (3) to add a different contour to the written melodic line, and (4) to allow the soloist the opportunity to add his particular creative skills to the composition. The combination of all of these factors added an air of personal freedom and an element of spontaneity to the composition. Baroque soloists would tend to play the same piece (especially the slow movements where there are

longer, slower notes which can be easily ornamented) in quite different manners. Even the same player would perform the same movement a little differently each time. So with this bit of personal freedom in the Baroque music came the challenge and responsibility to do something musically interesting and beautiful. Listen to recordings of some of the sonatas Handel wrote for oboe, violin, flute, and recorders. This will give you a better idea of the true Baroque style and of the freedoms in this music.

Measures 1-17 As was the case with many sonatas from this period, the piece has no introduction as the soloist and accompanist begin together. Prepare for this entrance by thinking of the tempo and then giving your accompanist a downbeat with a slight up-down motion of your instrument.

Illustrations 3, 4, 5, and 6 will introduce the suggested ornaments to you for measures 3, 6, 14, and 16.

ILLUSTRATION 3 WRITTEN   PLAYED

ILLUSTRATION 4 WRITTEN   PLAYED

ILLUSTRATION 5 WRITTEN   PLAYED

ILLUSTRATION 6 WRITTEN   PLAYED

Also remember, that as the slide and tongue move faster (as they must do when executing an ornament) the AIR must also move faster. Coordination of slide and tongue can be a problem, so work from slow to fast. Don't get ahead of yourself and waste time in your practice.

There are several places where two-note slurs are written. Remember to use the syllables "TAW DAW" for this grouping.

Be sure to play the "Ab's" in 3rd position and attack them with a relaxed tongue and good breath support.

Observe breath marks carefully — don't break the phrases! Take a full, deep breath each time you breathe (not so much, however, that you force the air in and tighten your throat). Observe the slight ritard. two measures before the "Allegro", breathe, then proceed with the "Allegro" section. The chord

in measure 17 must move ahead into the first chord at the "Allegro".

Measures 1-23 When you see **"**, this means to take an extra full breath. The phrase starting in measure 7 of the "Allegro" section is a long one. Take plenty of air where indicated, start softly, and save air if you can for the high "Ab" at the end of the phrase. You may leave out the "C" in measure 11

indicated ( ) and take a breath in this spot as you learn this movement at a slower tempo. Later as you increase the

tempo to ♩ =120, try to complete this entire phrase in one breath.

The ornament in measure 22 should be played as shown in Illustration 7.

ILLUSTRATION 7

WRITTEN

PLAYED

Measures 24-46 The accompaniment has the same melody in this section. It should be performed in the same style and both the top and bottom lines should be brought out.

Measures 47-68 This section starts in a style similar to the beginning of the "Allegro". To achieve a good sound on the accents, use more air than tongue. Beginning at measure 49 change the dynamic level and the style for contrast.

Measures 69-90 Begin this section with a full, accented sound. As a contrast measure 73 is legato in style. The sudden change in measure 85 is very effective and should come as a surprise to the listener. The building from this soft section creates an exciting and energetic ending.

As with the other Handel composition, there is an optional basso continuo part included for this solo. Remember that (when accompanying the trombone) the piano part should be played lightly for the best effect.

Largo and Allegro

George Frederic Handel
(1685-1759)

Introduction and Dance

musical terms

mässig — moderate, moderately
langsam — slow
schnell — quick

new notes

  **B♭** pedal — 1st Position

A pedal — 2nd Position

This is another contemporary composition by Robert Kehrberg. It is atonal (does not seem to have a clear tonal center) and is based on a tone row (a melody or series of notes using all the notes in a one octave chromatic scale). This method of composition was formulated by Arnold Schonberg in 1921 and is called the Twelve-Tone System.

The melodic lines are made up of motives (melodic bits and ideas) taken from this series of notes and the harmonies are built of chords combining these melodic motives. The tone row this piece is built on appears in measures 131 and 132 in the trombone part and appears altogether in the piano part in the last measure (this effect is called a tone cluster). The tone row can be played backwards (called retrograde) or in inversion (upside down) and in several other ways. Below are illustrated some of the possibilities.

ILLUSTRATION 8

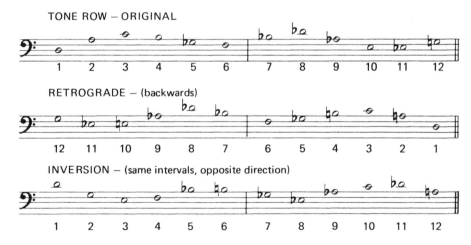

This piece also includes many of the other characteristics found in contemporary music such as:

1. Absence of key signatures requiring the use of accidentals.
2. Use of extreme dynamic levels. You will find "p" to "ff" as well as many crescendos and decrescendos in this selection.
3. Unusual or wide intervals. Intervals as large as minor ninths are used in "Introduction and Dance".
4. Extreme registers. This composition includes "A" below the staff to "A♭" above the staff.
5. Unusual rhythms or combinations of rhythms with accents in unfamiliar places in the measure. In measure

22 you'll see  and in many places

6. Changing meters. This piece changes from 4/4 to 3/4 briefly in two places — keep the ♩ constant. The metronome will help.

Measures 1-13 Always count to yourself to keep the rhythms clear in your mind. If you are having any problems, listen to the cassette to become more familiar with the part.

Throughout the piece the wide intervals are usually indicated to be played with the slide coming in for the higher note of the interval (making use of the compression in the slide).

Preparation 13 isolates the large intervals and gives you an opportunity to hear and practice them (first slowly then up to ♩=144).

PREPARATION 13

M.M. ♩=60-144

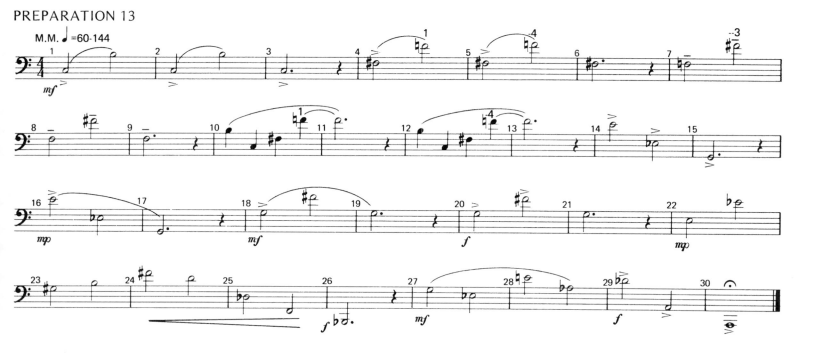

Measures 14-27   In measure 22 you have a new triplet which divides the half note into three equal parts.

$$\text{♩} = \overset{3}{♩\ ♩\ ♩}$$ Place the three notes equally throughout the first two beats of the measure. Another way you may think of this rhythm is:

Measures 28-61   The dance-like section begins in this measure. Listen carefully to the accompaniment interlude before your entrance to pick up the new tempo and watch for the change of meter in measure 34.

Practice slowly at first, then up to tempo, measures 38-41, 45-47, 49-55, and put extra weight on these accented notes with AIR — blow this air from the **beltline**.

Observe the extreme low notes (pedal "B♭" and "A") in measures 58, 70, and 82. Preparation 14 will help you gain security with these notes. When playing pedal notes relax your cheeks, but don't puff them extremely, and keep the corners gently in place. Blow a BIG, SLOW, SUSTAINED stream of air across the top lip and UP into the upper part of the cup of the mouthpiece. Don't blow hard — coax those pedal notes out.

PREPARATION 14

M.M. ♩=60

Measures 62-86   Interest is created in this section in the variety of things which happen: shorter notes with accents mixed with long, sustained, legato notes: extremely low notes and high "F♯" used together; and a range of dynamics from "p" to "ff". Watch carefully and bring out all these contrasts.

Measures 87-107   In this section you'll have an opportunity to display a big, intense, full sound and lots of energy. There are also numerous accents that must be played accurately.

Measures 108-133   This section starts like the beginning of the "Dance". This return to the original theme is called the recapitulation. End this piece with a big, full sound and

tremendous energy and drive. The tone cluster played by the piano in the last measure must sound almost like an explosion.

"Introduction and Dance" will present quite a challenge to the intermediate trombonist. The idea in presenting a piece of this difficulty is twofold — (1) to encourage you to reach new levels of proficiency and (2) to give you some idea of the kind of challenges found in the more advanced trombone literature (much of it is considerably more difficult than "Introduction and Dance").

We wish you enjoyment and many hours of personal satisfaction in your pursuit of mastery of the trombone.

Introduction and Dance

31

position chart
(Alternate positions are shown in parentheses)

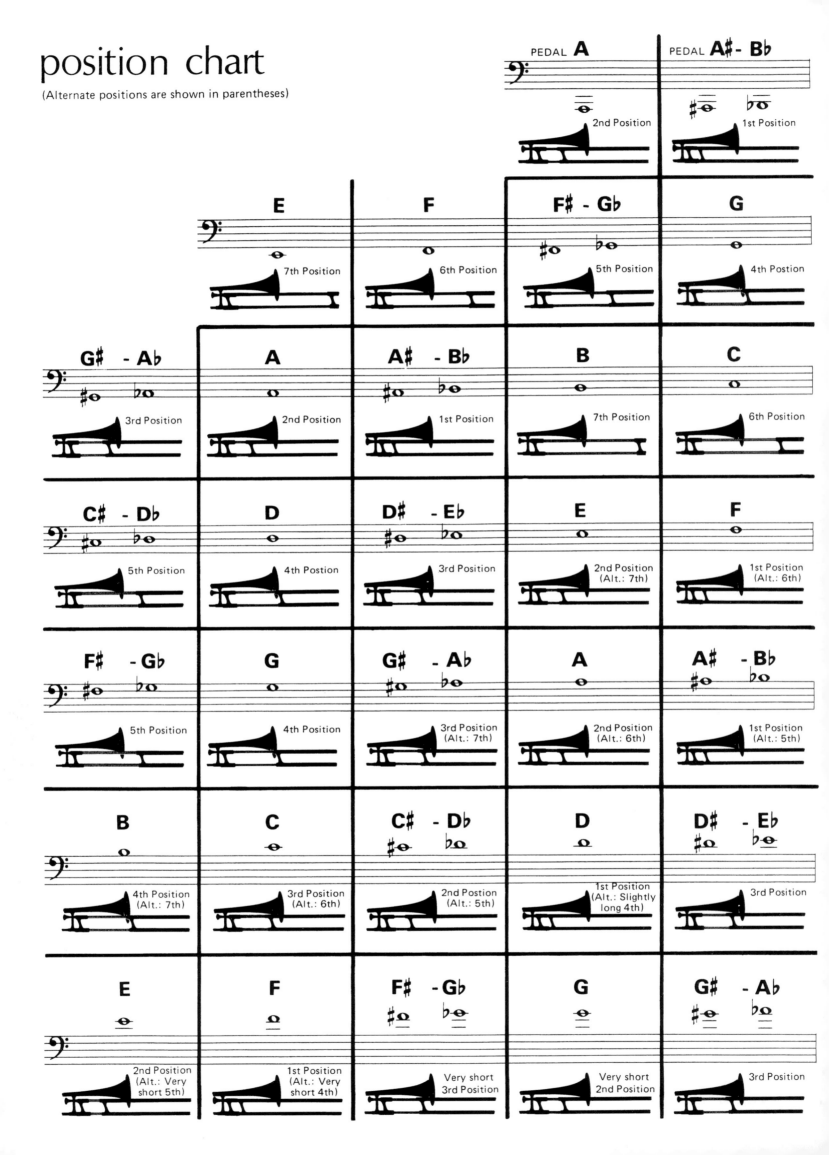